THE GIANT BOOK OF
CREATURES
OF THE NIGHT

JIM PIPE

COPPER BEECH BOOKS • BROOKFIELD, CONNECTICUT

CONTENTS

THE GIANT BOOK OF
CREATURES
OF THE NIGHT

© Aladdin Books Ltd 1998

Designed and produced by
Aladdin Books Ltd
28 Percy Street
London W1P 0LD

*First published in the United States
in 1998 by*
Copper Beech Books,
an imprint of
The Millbrook Press
2 Old New Milford Road
Brookfield, Connecticut 06804

Editor
Emma Wild
Design
David West
Children's Book Design
Designer
Flick Killerby
Illustrators
Rob Shone, Jonathon Pointer, Myke Taylor
— Wildlife Art Ltd, Roger Vlitos (enhanced photos),
Francis Phillipps, Karen Johnson, George Thompson,
David Wood — Wildlife Art Ltd, Darren Harvey —
Wildlife Art Ltd, Tony Bennett, Richard Orr, John
Rignall, Peter Barrett — Artist Partners,
Stella Robinson, Justine Peek, Gary Hincks,
Alan Male, Bootsy Collins, Roy Coombs, Philip
Weare, Norman Weaver, Tony Swift, James Field —
Simon Girling & Associates.

Printed in Belgium
All rights reserved
5 4 3 2 1

A copy of CIP data is kept on record
at the Library of Congress.
ISBN 0-7613-0777-X (trade hc.).
ISBN 0-7613-0858-X (lib. bdg.).

The author, Jim Pipe, is a writer and
editor of children's books.

The consultant, David Burnie, is a biologist
who writes for adults and children.

INTRODUCTION

Welcome to the secret world of creatures that go bump in the night. Read on, and feel your spine tingle as owls hoot from the darkness, squeaking vampire bats fly through your hair, and wolves howl at the moon. You will be amazed how these nighttime prowlers search for food and friends in almost complete darkness — without even a flashlight! In addition to all sorts of furry nighttime animals, watch out for heat-detecting snakes, beetles that glow in the dark, and razor-toothed sharks that hunt in the moonlight.

Because they have adapted to life with little or no light, many night creatures seem very strange to us humans, such as bushbabies with their huge eyes or bats with their hideous wrinkled faces. But some are *really* freaky. To find these weird and wonderful animals, look out for the amazed face (*above right*). For example, check out the fish with no eyes that lives in underground caves (page 29).

We've also picked out some of the most incredible features used by animals to get around at night — did you know that the duck-billed platypus has electric sensors in its bill (page 14)? Watch for the sign of the bat (*above left*).

You may be terrified by scratching noises outside the window or bright eyes glowing in the dark. But fear not. Many nocturnal creatures are shy, harmless animals that live at night to avoid large predators. Most are more scared of you than you are of them!

Cold-blooded reptiles, like the poisonous Gila monster, cannot control the temperature of their bodies the way mammals can. So some hunt at night to avoid overheating in the sun.

Gila monster

STAYING ALIVE

Many of the first mammals looked like today's shrews or possums. They lived in the age of the dinosaurs (*left*), and their warm-blooded bodies allowed them to be active at night when there was less threat from dinosaurs.

Today, small mammals, like the Australian jerboa, feed at night to avoid being eaten by predators that hunt during the day.

Jerboa

WHY LIVE IN THE DARK?

At nightfall, most animals are returning to the safety of their homes. But for some, life begins at sunset. These creatures are said to be "nocturnal." Some feed at night to avoid being eaten by predators or to avoid competition from bigger or smarter rivals. Creatures with slimy skins, like frogs (*below*), come out after dark to avoid the hot sun, which would dry out their moist skins.

WHOSE TURN TO EAT?
In parts of Africa, up to five kinds of driver ant can be found living in one area. They lead very similar lives, but each kind of ant is only active during a particular part of the day or night. In this way, they can all survive without competing with each other for food.

Tree frogs

Driver ants

Night Suckers
Some plants, such as honeysuckle and evening primrose, give off more of their sweet perfume at night. Night-flying moths and some bats can easily track down the nectar, which they suck out with their long tongues.

NOISES IN THE NIGHT
Most of us have been kept awake by strange noises in the dark. But did you know that many are messages being sent from one animal to another? Howler monkeys yell and owls hoot, wail, or shriek to tell others to "keep away" from their feeding grounds. Wolves howl to "talk" to others in their pack, and crickets chirp loudly to attract a mate.
Hyenas (right) *make all sorts of whoo-oops, giggles, yells, and cackles that sound like crazy laughter.*

This fish has no eyes because it spends its life in dark underground caves.

CONSTANT NIGHT
Many sea creatures live in darkness since the sun's rays cannot reach the deeper parts of the ocean. Like nocturnal animals, they often have special senses (page 29).

SILENT NIGHT HUNTERS
For predators like the leopard (*above*), the night is a great time to hunt. Its sharp senses and soft paws allow it to creep up on other animals. Night hunters can also pounce on sleeping prey.

NIGHT SENSES
Nocturnal animals have at least one sense — sight, hearing, taste, smell, or touch — which is especially good. Owls have great hearing, and large eyes for seeing well in the dark. Others have unusual powers that help them to locate their prey even if they can't see or hear them. Bats use the echoes from their high-pitched squeaks to catch insects in total darkness (page 18). All the animals below *have special night senses.*

Great horned owl

SMELL
Like many small mammals, tree shrews have a fantastic sense of smell.

SUPER SIGHT
Most cats have a special part to their eye that helps them see in the dark.

BLOOD SNIFFERS
Sharks can detect the blood of a wounded animal a mile away.

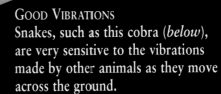

GOOD VIBRATIONS
Snakes, such as this cobra (*below*), are very sensitive to the vibrations made by other animals as they move across the ground.

SENSORS
Sharks can pick up electrical signals made by moving animals, using organs on their snouts.

BIG EYES
Many small night-living mammals, like this bushbaby, have huge eyes that let in more light in the dark.

THE BIG CATS

Big predators, like lions, can hunt or sleep whenever they like — most other animals are too terrified to attack them! But many cats, including your family pet, prefer to hunt in the dark. Cats have spongy footpads that allow them to walk quietly, so at night they can creep up on sleeping animals — a lot less effort than chasing after their prey!

Cats also have eyes that are specially adapted for seeing in the dark, and blind newborn kittens can sniff out where they live by using scent alone. A cat's whiskers are so sensitive to air currents that in tests they could detect and avoid obstacles even when blindfolded.

Puma

Leopard

LION LARDERS
Pumas, also called mountain lions or cougars, are American big cats. They hunt after dark, by leaping out on animals and breaking their necks. They eat as much as they can, then drag the remains to a hiding place, where they cover them with leaves, ready for the next meal.

Jaguar

THE CAT'S WHISKERS
The whiskers of a cat are special hairs that are highly sensitive to touch. As well as helping cats to find their way around in the dark, the whiskers are a very important tool when the cat is attacking its victim.

As the cat pounces, it will bring its whiskers forward so that, in the split second before catching its prey, it can sense exactly where the victim is.

Whiskers can also tell a cat which way the wind is blowing.

MIDNIGHT SWIMMERS
The beautiful and powerful South American jaguar hunts at night for deer and other mammals. This big cat is a great swimmer and scoops fish out of the water with its sharp claws. It even hunts crocodiles! It drags them from the water, flipping them over, and kills them by ripping their soft underbelly.

Lynx

LYNX
Many cats show others they are angry by waving their tail. But the night-hunting lynx wiggles its long black ear-tufts to tell other lynxes to stay clear.

ALL THE BETTER TO SEE YOU WITH
Some animals, such as cats and crocodiles, use a special part of their eye to help them see at night. You may have seen a cat's eyes glow eerily when they look into a light. This is caused by a mirrorlike layer of cells called the tapetum. This bounces light back onto sensors in the cat's eye, giving it a second chance to see.

Other creatures have extra large eyes to let in more light. Imagine what you'd look like if you had night vision!

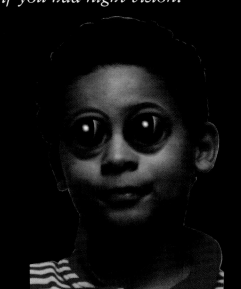

LEOPARDS
Leopards are great night hunters — they have even dragged sleeping humans from houses without waking anyone else! A leopard will patiently stalk an animal for hours before it seizes its prey with its claws in a short, violent charge. Though only the size of a big dog, leopards will eat anything, from worms and berries to antelopes weighing 440 pounds.

SNOW LEOPARD
The snow leopard lives high in the Himalaya Mountains. It has fur up to 4 inches thick to protect it from the cold. It hunts at night, stalking herds of goats and deer while they are feeding or sleeping. Sometimes, it attacks its prey with a flying tackle from 15 feet away.

Snow leopard

THE KING OF THE JUNGLE
Lions are most successful when they hunt just after dark or before the sun rises. Like other cats, they have large eyes designed for night hunting. They band together, not just to work as a team to catch food, but also to defend their food supply against nighttime gangs of hyenas.

Lion

SOFT-FOOTED TIGERS
Tigers like to hunt alone and at night. They are completely noiseless and will inch slowly toward their prey before bounding the last few yards and leaping on their victims. In a year, a tiger kills an average 30 animals.

Tiger

Serval

SPRINGING SERVALS
Like pumas and leopards, the spotted serval sometimes has an all-black coat — perfect for night hunting. It is so fast and agile, it can even catch flying birds.

Wild hunting dog

Gray wolf

Jackal

WILD DOGS

Wolves (left), coyotes, and dingoes are wild members of the dog family. They all hunt at night, whether alone, in pairs, or in packs. Though famous for their eerie nighttime howling, wolves and coyotes communicate in lots of different ways, using their faces and tails, and by nuzzling up against each other. As active night hunters, members of the dog family have excellent vision and a keen sense of smell.

NIGHT OF THE JACKAL

By day, jackals usually hide in long grass and come out at night to hunt. They often follow lions in the hope that they can share the kill, but they also hunt their own food, such as rats, mice, and even large pythons.

Dingo

Coyote

A HOWL IN THE DARK

Many other meat-eating mammals have adapted to a nocturnal life, such as foxes, raccoons, wild dogs, and badgers. Some predators come out at night because it's cooler, and others because prey such as rabbits and mice are active. Most have a good sense of smell and excellent hearing, and like dogs, will swivel their ears to pinpoint where a sound is coming from. Once upon a time, our human ancestors may also have done this (but unfortunately, wiggling your ears won't improve your hearing now!).

Brown bears

DOG, MONGOOSE, OR MONSTER? Night-hunting hyenas look like dogs, but are in fact related to mongooses. In African myth, witches were said to ride around on them. They still have an evil reputation because they feed on dead animals and steal prey from lions and wild dogs. Their jaws are strong enough to crunch through a giraffe's hip bone. Once they have caught their prey, hyenas will eat it until it dies.

BROWN BEARS

Because they need to eat a lot to keep their warm bodies going, many mammals must feed whenever they can. Brown bears eat day and night, and will devour anything from honey to fish. They can even be found raiding garbage cans in search of kitchen scraps.

RACCOONS

Raccoons are mammals with a black band of hair around the eyes that looks like a mask. They live both on the ground and in trees, and many now live in towns. They are unafraid of humans and will even beg for food. Raccoons usually hunt for food at night and stay in their dens during the day. They walk like bears on four feet, and are excellent swimmers that can catch crabs, fish, and frogs.

BADGERS

Badgers have thick bodies and paws with strong claws that are perfect for digging the burrows that they hide in during the day. The badger feeds at night, on anything from rabbits to slugs, wasps, and berries.

Badgers

MONGOOSES

Mongooses are small nocturnal mammals that are famous for hunting snakes. Though snake poison can kill them, mongooses are so fast that they can seize and kill a snake before the snake has the chance to bite them. Mongooses also eat birds' eggs, mice, birds, and other small animals.

Mongoose

DESERT MAMMALS

Mammals that live in the desert often have amazing hearing to help them at night. The fennec fox (3) has big ears to help funnel sound into its eardrum. The flaps can be swiveled around like a dog's. The desert is a scary place for small creatures like the hedgehog (2) and desert hare (1) — there is nowhere to hide. They use their hearing to detect predators. Part of a kangaroo rat's (4) ears are like air-filled balloons. They can pick out the low sounds made by slithering snakes.

Because we live such noisy lives, surrounded by cars and other machines, humans will probably never develop large ears for night hearing (*right*)!

EVENING SWIMMERS

Otters are expert swimmers with webbed feet and waterproof fur. They can stay underwater for three or four minutes. At night, they slip out of their burrows to catch fish and frogs.

Otter

FOXES

These cunning night hunters have always raided farmyards for chickens. Now that many live in towns, they have been blamed for killing pet cats. This is usually untrue, but they will pick up dead cats they find on the road.

Red fox

NIGHT RAID!

Your yard and local park also come alive after dark. Many animals are attracted to towns by scraps of food or other garbage, or by the warmth of our homes. In 1832, even New York City was described as a "huge pigsty" because bands of wild pigs roamed the streets eating the garbage! Even in our homes we are not alone, as nighttime nibblers such as rats, mice, cockroaches, and beetles go about their business.

ANIMAL PROWLERS IN A NORTH EUROPEAN BACKYARD
1 Rabbit 2 Domestic cat 3 Common garden spider 4 Common slug 5 and 19 Garden snails 6 and 11 Common frog 7 Fox's pawprint 8 Badgers rubbing against each other as a way of saying hello 9 Gray heron 10 Tawny owl 12 Daubenton's bat 13 Common shrew 14 Hedgehog 15 Fox 16 Mole 17 Cat and hedgehog 18 Woodlouse 20 Elephant hawk moth 21 and 22 Long-eared bats. Did you also spot the roe deer in the park?

Duck-billed platypuses are one of a group of animals called monotremes — the only mammals that lay eggs. These eggs are soft and rubbery, and the young hatch after two weeks.

DUCK-BILLED DIVER

This curious mammal hunts in the dark in the slow-flowing parts of streams and rivers. It dives down to the bottom and pokes around in the mud with its bill. But the platypus is deaf and blind underwater, so it uses special sensors in its bill that produce an electrical field. These tell it where its favorite foods — shrimps and worms — are hiding in the mud.

SINKING ECHIDNAS

This monotreme feeds on ants and termites at night with its tubelike muzzle.

If disturbed, the short-beaked echidna digs down into the soil so fast that it looks like a ship sinking — leaving a hungry attacker face-to-face with a ball of prickly spines.

THE TINY PILBARA

This marsupial can weigh as little as half an ounce, so it's not surprising that it prefers to feed at night to avoid predators.

SLEEPING KOALAS

Night-living koalas eat leaves from only a few smooth-barked eucalyptus trees. This diet means these marsupials sleep for 18 out of every 24 hours — most of their energy is spent digesting the tough leaves.

Koala

Wombat

BURROWING WOMBATS

Wombats live in areas with little rainfall in southern Australia. They only come out of their burrows at night, to avoid losing water from their bodies in the sun. Their burrows are up to 100 feet long and 20 inches wide.

TOUGH GUYS?

One cuddly-looking possum, the cuscus, can be very aggressive. If a cuscus meets another, they will threaten each other by snarling, hissing, and standing upright. To tell other possums to keep clear, a cuscus dribbles spit onto branches nearby or urinates on the ground below its feeding area.

Cuscus

UNDERGROUND, OVERGROUND

The marsupial mole has short, stubby limbs designed for burrowing, and its snout forms a hornlike shield that protects its head while it is digging. Since it spends most of its time below ground and has no eyes that work, the mole doesn't care whether it is day or night!

Sugar gliders come out at night to feed on sweet syrup from eucalyptus trees. If disturbed, they leap into the darkness and can glide up to 300 feet through the air. But when they land, they bump into the trees, then hang on desperately with their claws.

Marsupial moles feed on insects such as burrowing grubs. They live in the central deserts of Australia.

Sugar glider

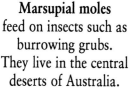

Antechinus

LONE MARSUPIAL MOTHERS
After mating, the males of one kind of antechinus die within five days, leaving the females to bring up the young on their own.

VIRGINIA OPOSSUM
This North American marsupial has a cat-sized body and is a great climber (left). It has a tail like a monkey that can grip branches like a hand. This opossum lives on fruit, insects, and dead animals, and has very sharp hearing. Its naked ears are always moving as it tracks the sounds of other animals.

FURRY JUMPERS
Kangaroos (*below*) have powerful back legs and a tail that they use to balance with when hopping. The kangaroo can hop at speeds of up to 40 mph over short distances. It also has enough spring in its legs to jump right over the head of an adult human.

Tree kangaroos
Amazingly, some kangaroos live in trees. Unlike other kangaroos, they move their back feet separately — otherwise, it would be very hard for them to climb!

Virginia opossum

Red kangaroo

POUCHED PROWLERS

Animals like kangaroos and koalas are also active at night. They are mammals like us, but give birth to tiny young that develop in a pouch outside their mother's body. These creatures, called marsupials, use the cover of darkness to travel between feeding and resting sites. Kangaroos, for example, feed during the day in the winter months, but in the hot summer season, they rest in the day and search for food at night. Marsupials have a good sense of smell, and mark their areas with stinky dung and urine.

Tasmanian devil

KANGAROO POUCHES
When female kangaroos give birth to a joey (baby), it measures just an inch long, and must crawl up its mother's belly until it reaches her pouch.
Here it attaches itself to a nipple and feeds on her milk. The joey leaves its mother's pouch for the first time after six months. But for the next couple of months, it will still hop back into the pouch if it is scared.

SCARY NAME, ROTTEN HUNTER
One scary-looking, meat-eating marsupial is called the Tasmanian devil, because of its strong jaws and sharp teeth. But many of these "devils" are such poor hunters that they must often eat the bodies of dead animals to survive.

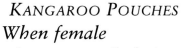

FURRY FORAGERS

Many of the mammals around at the time of the dinosaurs died out when stronger, smarter rivals such as monkeys came along. But some ancient mammals, such as lorises, tarsiers, and bushbabies, avoided competition by living at night. Many developed huge eyes and ears. In fact, the bushbaby is so careful about its ears, it always folds them to avoid snagging them when it jumps from branch to branch. Other nocturnal mammals developed special features to defend themselves.

Slender loris

Tarsier

NIGHT POISONERS
Skunks may look very cute with their black and white fur. But if frightened or attacked, they can spray a powerful mix of chemicals up to 13 feet away. These chemicals produce a terrible stink, which remains for days on whatever has been sprayed. The spray can also cause blindness if it hits the eyes of an attacker.

Polecats and pine martens also produce chemical sprays to defend themselves. The duck-billed platypus has a venom-producing spur on its rear ankle that is poisonous enough to kill a dog.

Pine marten

Skunks sleep during the day in underground dens lined with dry leaves.

FINDING ITS WAY HOME
Before the bushbaby (*right*) sets out into the night, it performs a strange ritual — it cups its hands and urinates on them. In this way, it makes sure that every step of its journey leaves a smelly reminder to guide it back home. Don't try this yourself!

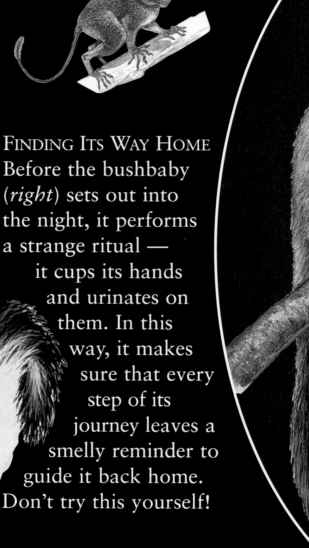

Armor-Plated Pangolins
Unlike most mammals, pangolins are protected by a covering of hornlike body scales. When they curl up, they are protected by a natural suit of armor, which can only be crushed by the powerful jaws of a hyena or a lion.

WILD BOARS
If you hear a snuffling sound in the dark from the bushes, it may be a wild boar. These intelligent animals have sharp hearing and sight, and "talk" to each other constantly with loud grunts, chirps, and squeaks.

GREEDY GERBILS?

Like many small mammals, gerbils are nocturnal to avoid losing water from their bodies in the sun's heat. Most of the food they eat is dry, so they leave seeds outside their burrows to soak up water from the moist night air. They also eat juicy animals, like snails.

Gerbil

It's easy to see how the **kangaroo rat** *got its name with those legs!*

HEDGEHOG HUNTERS

These small mammals are best known for defending themselves with their prickly coat by rolling up into a ball. But they are also ferocious hunters — they can even kill and eat animals as large as chickens. They are fearless snake-killers too, as they are not hurt by snake poison.

WHISTLING VOLES

Voles are micelike rodents that feed by day and night. Each type of vole has its own call — the Brandt's vole, for example, whistles loudly at other voles.

Lemming

THE LEMMING EXPLOSION

People once believed that when the population of these rodents got too large, they would commit mass suicide by jumping over cliffs. This is untrue, but the number of lemmings often rises suddenly every four years.

HARD-WORKING AARDVARK

The aardvark uses its claws to rip open termite mounds. It licks up the termites with its tongue, which can be 18 inches long! In a few minutes, it can also dig a deep hole to escape from its enemies. It sleeps in its burrow during the day and hunts after dark.

An **aardvark** can tell whether an insect mound is occupied just by listening!

Red howler monkey

MOLES

Moles are active both day and night. They rely on touch to guide them through their system of tunnels — the star-nosed mole's nose is divided into 22 highly sensitive tentacles. When moles do come to the surface, it is usually to collect materials for their nests. One mole nest found was made entirely of potato chip packets!

SHREWS

Busy shrews munch on insects and worms by day and night. They are in danger of starving if they stop eating for longer than an hour.

The **tree shrew** is perhaps the closest relative to the ancient mammals that lived at the time of the dinosaurs.

Star-nosed mole

HOWLER MONKEYS

Howler monkeys (right) *are named after the loud, roaring noises they make at sunrise. A group of howlers can be heard up to 3 miles away.*

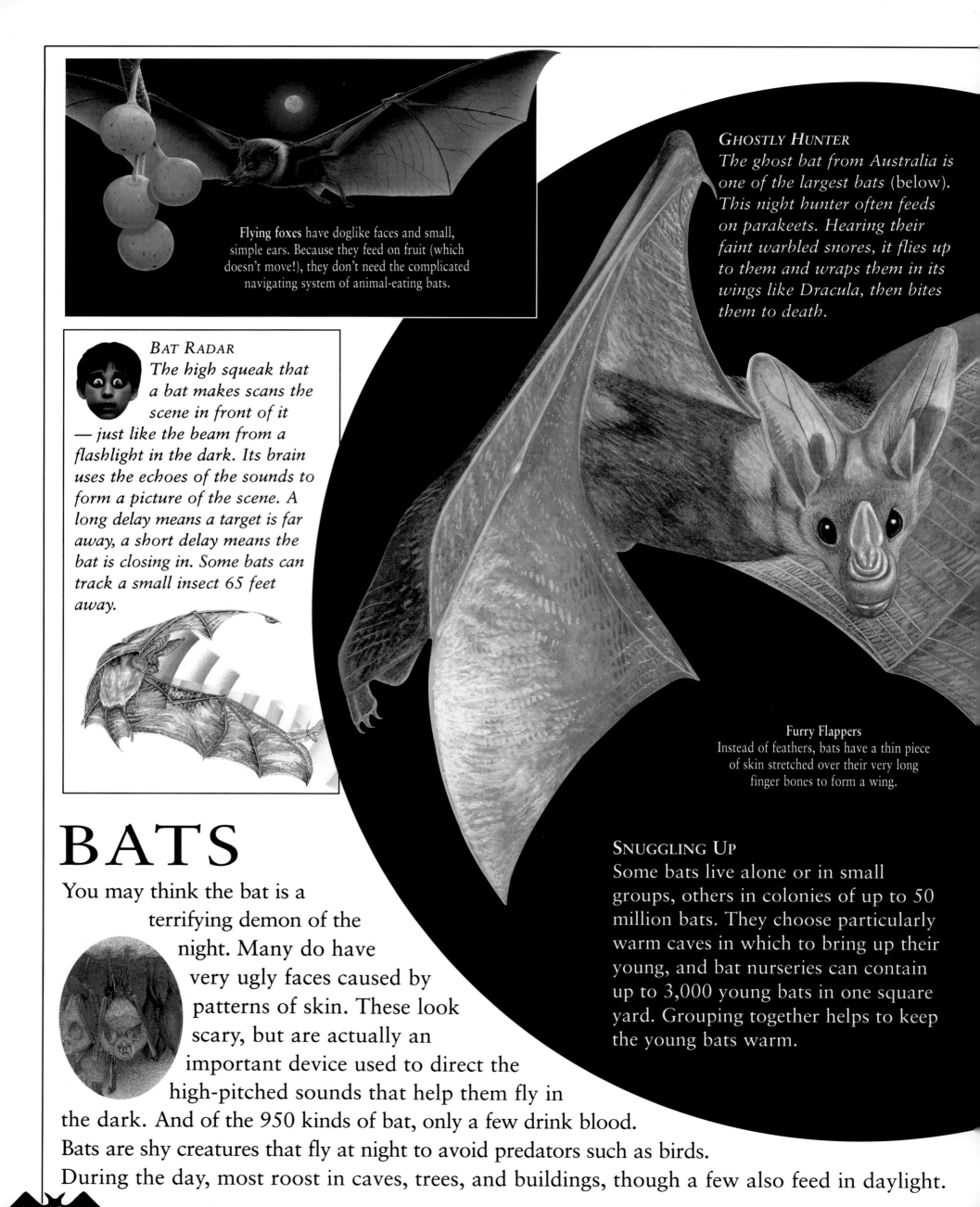

Flying foxes have doglike faces and small, simple ears. Because they feed on fruit (which doesn't move!), they don't need the complicated navigating system of animal-eating bats.

BAT RADAR
The high squeak that a bat makes scans the scene in front of it — just like the beam from a flashlight in the dark. Its brain uses the echoes of the sounds to form a picture of the scene. A long delay means a target is far away, a short delay means the bat is closing in. Some bats can track a small insect 65 feet away.

GHOSTLY HUNTER
The ghost bat from Australia is one of the largest bats (below). This night hunter often feeds on parakeets. Hearing their faint warbled snores, it flies up to them and wraps them in its wings like Dracula, then bites them to death.

Furry Flappers
Instead of feathers, bats have a thin piece of skin stretched over their very long finger bones to form a wing.

SNUGGLING UP
Some bats live alone or in small groups, others in colonies of up to 50 million bats. They choose particularly warm caves in which to bring up their young, and bat nurseries can contain up to 3,000 young bats in one square yard. Grouping together helps to keep the young bats warm.

BATS

You may think the bat is a terrifying demon of the night. Many do have very ugly faces caused by patterns of skin. These look scary, but are actually an important device used to direct the high-pitched sounds that help them fly in the dark. And of the 950 kinds of bat, only a few drink blood.
Bats are shy creatures that fly at night to avoid predators such as birds.
During the day, most roost in caves, trees, and buildings, though a few also feed in daylight.

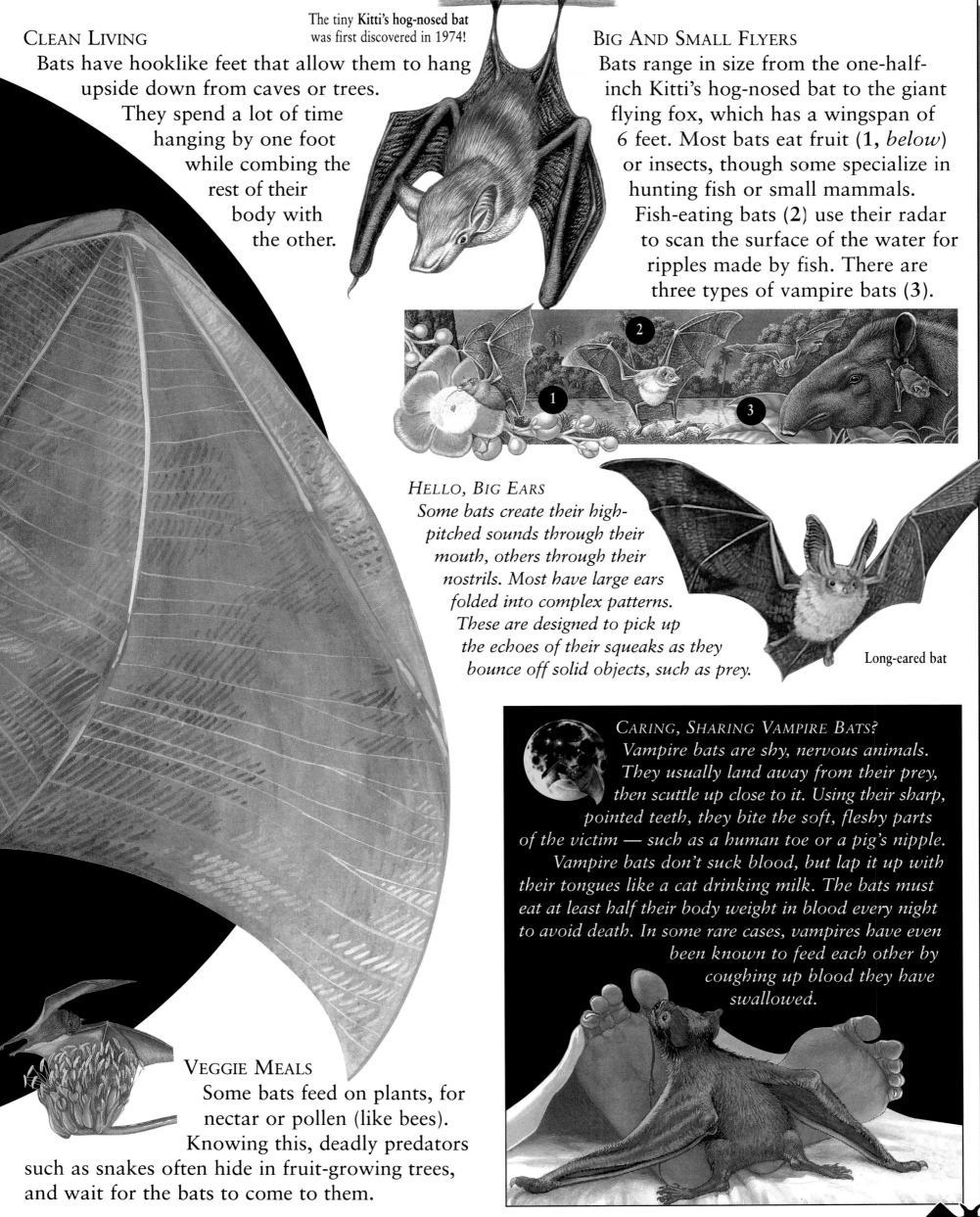

CLEAN LIVING

Bats have hooklike feet that allow them to hang upside down from caves or trees. They spend a lot of time hanging by one foot while combing the rest of their body with the other.

The tiny **Kitti's hog-nosed bat** was first discovered in 1974!

BIG AND SMALL FLYERS

Bats range in size from the one-half-inch Kitti's hog-nosed bat to the giant flying fox, which has a wingspan of 6 feet. Most bats eat fruit (**1**, *below*) or insects, though some specialize in hunting fish or small mammals. Fish-eating bats (**2**) use their radar to scan the surface of the water for ripples made by fish. There are three types of vampire bats (**3**).

HELLO, BIG EARS

Some bats create their high-pitched sounds through their mouth, others through their nostrils. Most have large ears folded into complex patterns. These are designed to pick up the echoes of their squeaks as they bounce off solid objects, such as prey.

Long-eared bat

VEGGIE MEALS

Some bats feed on plants, for nectar or pollen (like bees). Knowing this, deadly predators such as snakes often hide in fruit-growing trees, and wait for the bats to come to them.

CARING, SHARING VAMPIRE BATS?

Vampire bats are shy, nervous animals. They usually land away from their prey, then scuttle up close to it. Using their sharp, pointed teeth, they bite the soft, fleshy parts of the victim — such as a human toe or a pig's nipple. Vampire bats don't suck blood, but lap it up with their tongues like a cat drinking milk. The bats must eat at least half their body weight in blood every night to avoid death. In some rare cases, vampires have even been known to feed each other by coughing up blood they have swallowed.

NIGHT OWLS

Only a few birds are active at night. They rest in trees and bushes during the day, relying on the colors and patterns of their feathers to blend in with leaves and tree bark. As darkness falls, they take to the air and begin to hunt. These night birds can even catch flying insects, and some, such as nightjars, have special bristles on their beaks to stop their prey from slipping away. The best-known night flyers are the owls, with their large, often brightly colored eyes, and excellent hearing.

Eagle owl

SILENT FLYERS

Many owls have soft, velvety feathers that allow them to fly silently and pounce on their victims without being heard. They grasp the prey in their feet, using their sharp, curved claws. Owls' most common victims are mice, voles, and small birds, but some hunt fish, shrimp, and even prickly hedgehogs.

Owl pellets
Owl prey is usually swallowed whole, and parts such as fur, bones, feathers, and insect wings are coughed up in the form of neat pellets (*above*).

HEAD TURNERS

Owl eyes are one hundred times more sensitive to light than human eyes. But their ears are just as amazing. Sitting on its perch, a barn owl listens out for the slightest squeak or rustle. It can tell the height of a sound source exactly, because one of its earholes is slightly higher than the other.

Its hearing is also helped by the saucer-shaped ruff of tightly packed feathers around its face, which channels sound into its earholes. Finally, an owl can swivel its head right around without having to change position. You might find this useful if you wanted to chat in class to the person behind you!

Snowy owl

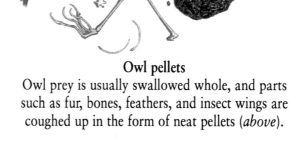

WORLD OF OWLS

There are 150 types of owl living all over the world. Among the largest are eagle, great gray, and snowy owls. Eagle owls can even kill small deer. Snowy owls hunt using the night lights of the northern summer and catch prey as big as geese or hares. The tiny elf owl has a body just 5 inches long. It lives in the deserts of North America and nests in holes drilled by woodpeckers in giant cacti.

Great gray owl

Horned owl — its tufts are not ears, but feathers used to signal to other owls.

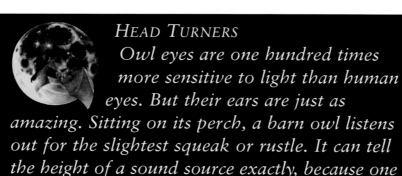

THE NIGHT SNIFFER

Not all nocturnal birds are flying hunters. The kiwi is a flightless bird that lives in forests. Though slow, it had no natural enemies before cats and dogs were brought to New Zealand. It is also one of the few night birds that uses smell rather than sight to find its food. Its nostrils are at the tip of its bill, and it spends the night probing the forest floor, sniffing out worms, insects, and fruit.

THE TWILIGHT ZONE

The bat hawk hunts in the twilight hours. It grabs bats with its feet and swallows them whole while it is still flying!

INSECT GOBBLERS

Nighthawks and nightjars hunt insects at night. They open their huge mouths as they fly and gobble up mosquitoes and moths in their path.

One **nightjar** wedges itself between rocks to hide during the day.

A **tawny owl** swoops on a mouse!

Albatross

DANCING FEET

Some birds feed both at night and during the day. Seabirds such as the albatross hunt during the day, but also feed on the small fish that come to the water's surface at night.

As they hunt close to the water, storm petrels skip across the water on dancing feet, scooping up fish and animal plankton. However, these birds are badly designed for moving on land. To avoid land-living predators, they nest in underground burrows, which they enter and leave under the cover of darkness.

THE CURIOUS KAKAPO

This rare night bird, a kind of parrot, can't fly like other birds. It can only climb trees and then glide back to the ground! It normally travels along the ground, clearing tracks through the undergrowth. It has a strange booming call, and feeds on wild berries and nectar.

Kakapo

THE LONGEST NIGHT

In winter, the days become shorter and the nights longer. But imagine living near the South Pole, where there is constant darkness in the winter months. Male emperor penguins spend this time looking after the eggs laid by their mates. Hundreds huddle together for warmth in the freezing cold.

Emperor penguin

Adélie penguin

A CROAK OF LOVE

In spring, male frogs and toads gather at their breeding ponds and call out to the females. They make loud croaking and booming noises by pumping air into special pouches on their throats. Females respond to their cries and come hopping or crawling to the pond where the males are. But if they detect a predator nearby, such as a snake, the males suddenly become very quiet indeed! Each type of frog has its own call, and scientists can often identify frogs more easily by their call than by their appearance.

Marbled reed frog

HOME-SHARING REPTILES

Tuataras look like lizards, but are in fact living fossils — animals that have not changed for 200 million years. They now survive only on a few islands off New Zealand. Many share their burrows with seabirds. While the birds are out during the day, the tuataras rest. On their return, the tuataras leave in search of food.

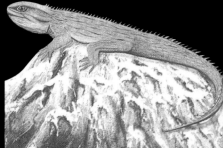

KEEPING THEIR SKINS SLIMY

Frogs and other amphibians, such as newts and toads, breathe partly through their skins. The only way they can do this is to keep their skins moist, so in hot countries they must avoid the fierce heat of the midday sun and feed at night.

CROCODILES

Using infrared cameras, scientists have recently discovered that crocodiles (left and below) are very active at night. Unlike some reptiles, they can easily cool down in the hot sun by going for a swim. But during the night, they can travel farther from water in search of prey without their bodies overheating.

HEAT-SEEKING SENSORS

All snakes are sensitive to heat. But some, such as bushmasters (right), *have special pits between their eyes and nostrils that allow them to pinpoint prey in the dark. They can detect heat from a mouse up to 12 inches away, or from a larger animal or human, several feet away.*

The heat-seeking image is combined in the brain with the image from the snake's eyes, so it can strike with deadly accuracy. Although you can't see or hear these snakes slithering toward you in the dark, they know exactly where you are!

Heat-seeking pit

FORKED TONGUES

The two forks in a snake's tongue allow it to smell in "stereo," in the same way that our two eyes and two ears help us to judge how far away things are. By picking up scents in the air and then licking the smelling organ in its mouth, a snake can work out where its prey has been. As mice often re-use the same routes each night, snakes can sniff out a good spot to ambush them.

Cobra

Bushmaster

NIGHT CRAWLERS

Many reptiles that live in the desert, like this chuckwalla (right), *hunt at night because their bodies would overheat in the hot midday sun.*

NIGHT SLITHERERS

Warm-blooded birds and mammals are not the only animals active at night. Slithery creatures, such as frogs, toads, and slugs, like dark, moist conditions because they need to keep their bodies damp. Many reptiles rest at night because they cannot keep their bodies warm enough to move about, but others are specially adapted for night hunting — especially snakes. They have an amazing sense of smell and can track other animals even when they can't be seen, by feeling vibrations on the ground.

The **egg-eating snake** is active at night, when the egg's parents may be asleep or resting.

KEEPING OUT OF THE SUN

Some desert-living reptiles, like this tortoise (above), *rest in cool burrows during the day, then come out at night to feed.*

EGG LAYING

Though they spend their lives at sea, turtles lay their eggs on land. Because they cannot move easily out of the water, they usually come ashore at night to avoid land-living predators.

A turtle burying its eggs in the sand.

AFRICAN DUSK

At night, the open grasslands of Africa are a dangerous place to sleep, especially when there is a leopard in the area. Some animals, such as baboons, sleep in the trees. Others seek safety in numbers, resting in large herds in the hope that their combined eyes and ears will detect any nearby predators.

Crocodiles and lions are often active at night, but if there is a fresh kill by the water's edge, lions will normally wait their turn, since even they cannot compete with hungry crocodiles.

NOCTURNAL ANIMALS OF THE AFRICAN GRASSLANDS
1 Eagle owl 2 Leopard 3 Scorpion 4 Marbled reed frog 5 Grasshopper 6 Lions and crocodiles 7 Elephant and giraffe herds 8 Banded mongoose 9 Spring hare 10 Pack of hyenas hunt a wildebeest 11 Baboons 12 Red-billed hornbill 13 Hippo passes termite mounds 14 Greater galago 15 Egg-eating snake

SCENT POWER

Although they have large eyes, moths also navigate by using their antennae to pick up scents in the air. The female emperor moth releases smells that can attract a male up to 3 miles away!

Antennae

Oleander hawk moth

EYE SPOTS

Flying at night helps moths to avoid birds that will eat them. They are usually colored like bark or tree leaves so that they can hide during the day. Some have large eye spots on their wings. When a moth flashes its wings, predators are startled because the spots look like the eyes of a bigger animal, giving the moth time to escape.

A Clifton nonpareil moth tries to escape from a bat.

Death's head hawk moth

RADAR JAMMERS

To avoid being eaten by bats, moths will execute a series of rolls, loops, and power dives to get away (*left*). But the tiger moth escapes by creating high-pitched sounds that confuse the bat's tracking system — a bit like jamming its radar.

Emperor moths

BED TIME BUGS

Can you imagine the sound of cockroaches scuttling to a hiding place in your house? Insects can be found everywhere after dark — even our homes are full of beetle larvae chomping through carpets or making strange ticking noises from the woodwork, and book lice munching on fungi in our books. Outside, male crickets and grasshoppers (*left*) sing noisily through the night to attract females, while other insects rely on scents in the wind to find their mate.

PREDATOR AND PREY

Praying mantises are fierce insect hunters that grasp their prey with armlike forelegs. To avoid being eaten themselves, they have a single ear to detect bats.

LIGHTING UP THE NIGHT

Fireflies and glowworms are actually kinds of beetle. The female fireflies attract mates by flashing their tails. The glow is made by a chemical reaction that gives off energy in the form of light.

The light from fireflies is so bright that the people who live in regions where fireflies occur tie three or four fireflies to their ankles. This provides enough light to follow a trail in the dark. Glowworms were once used as lamps.

Female **fireflies** flash signals to the males.

A Sticky Trap
The bolas spider traps moths with a cunning device. It uses special glands in its body to create a ball of sticky gum. Then it spins a line of silk about 2 inches long and attaches the ball to the end. The gum has a sweet smell that lures moths close enough for the spider to catch them.

Hairy-Legged Hunters
The bird-eating spider from South America also likes to hunt at night. Its legs are covered in fine hairs that pick up vibrations in the air from the movement of other animals.

Bird-eating spider

Ambush Tactics
As night falls, a trapdoor spider will gently raise the silken door at the entrance to its burrow. Any insect that comes too near is seized by a lightning swoop of the spider's front legs. The prey is then dragged inside and eaten. Scorpions also hunt at night by waiting for prey to pass by their lairs. They catch prey with pincerlike claws or stun them with the poisonous sting on their tail.

Trapdoor spider

Poisonous Centipedes
Centipedes are nocturnal creepy crawlies with bodies divided into many segments, each with a pair of legs. One type of centipede is one foot long and has curved, horny claws that act like fangs. Its sting is poisonous enough to kill a small child.

Going Underground
For insects that live underground, day and night are the same. As termites (right) are so pale, they are easily killed by sunshine. So even during the day, they travel underground. If they do move above ground, they build covered runways. Most termites are blind and live in huge colonies. Their nests can be 30 feet high and have special chimneys that suck warm air up and keep the nest cool.

———— Air tunnel to cool the termite nest

Crazy Rhythms
Some underground creatures talk to each other using sound. Termites, for example, will drum out a warning if a predator approaches. African mole rats (above) use their head to thump against the burrow walls. Each species has its own rhythm to tell others to keep away, and to find a mate. Moles, however, have no external ears and leave scent markings to let other moles know where they are.

MOONLIT WATERS

The oceans are busy 24 hours a day. At sunset, billions of minute animals, known as plankton, rise to the surface to feed on tiny plants. They are followed by small fish who feed on the plankton, hunted in turn by larger fish and sharks. Many creatures living in the ocean deep see no daylight at all, as the sun's rays cannot reach below 650 feet.

Flying fish often feed at night.

Goblin shark

Megamouth shark

MOONLIGHT HUNTERS
Some sharks hunt in the moonlight using their sharp hearing, good sense of smell, and ability to pick up electrical signals from moving prey. The whitetip reef shark, for example, cruises around slowly for food during the night, and spends the day sleeping on the ocean floor or in caves, to avoid being spotted.

GOBLIN SHARK
The goblin shark lives at the bottom of the ocean. It uses its long sensitive snout to detect prey nearby.

Whitetip reef shark

MEGAMOUTH
Some sharks living in the deepest parts of the ocean make their own light. The jaws of the megamouth shark give out a silvery glow — probably to attract tasty shrimp.

LANTERN SHARKS
Lantern sharks (right) glow in the water, thanks to a luminous slime on their skin. This glow may attract prey or help the sharks to keep out of each other's way when swimming together.

Sand tiger shark

TIGER SHARK
The tiger shark is a deadly night stalker. During the day, it swims lazily about, but at night it moves inshore to shallow waters to feed. Tiger sharks can open their jaws extra wide, so their bite is enormous. Their teeth have sharp points and sawlike edges that are just perfect for slicing up prey into chunks they can swallow.

GLOWING WONDERS

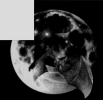

Fish, squid, and jellyfish fill the ocean deep with their own shimmering light. Special chemicals in their bodies give off light when exposed to oxygen in the water. One tiny relative of the sea squirt groups together in huge numbers to form tubular colonies up to 30 feet long — big enough for a human diver to swim into (right). There are even reports of these glowing colonies being torpedoed by submarines because they looked like enemy ships on radar!

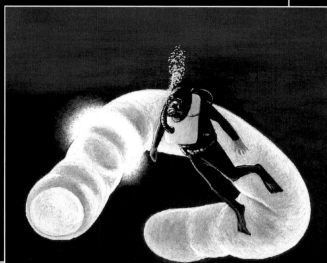

A DARK WORLD

To search for food in the dark, deep-sea world is almost impossible, so fish living near the ocean floor create their own light to catch prey. The hatchet fish uses luminous patches inside its mouth to guide smaller fish in, and the rat-trap fish has a glowing red light below one of its eyes.

ONE BIG GULP

The gulper eel gets its victim's attention with a light on the end of its tail. The gulper also has a huge mouth and a stomach that can swallow a fish up to three times its own size, so it can eat anything that comes its way!

All these fish live in the chilly, dark world of the ocean deep:

1 Snipe eel 2 Hatchet fish 3 Rat-trap fish
4 Linophryne 5 Deep-sea shrimp 6 Frilled shark
7 Gulper eel 8 Angler fish 9 Viper fish 10 Squid
11 Lantern fish 12 Lamptotoxus 13 Opisthoproctus
14 Laslognathus

Shrimp

A LITTLE NIGHT MUSIC

At night, the sea is also full of strange sounds — turtles calling, and lobsters and shrimps scuttling on the seafloor. You can even hear a sound like a gunshot — when the pistol shrimp snaps its claws together.

SHARP-EYED PIRANHAS

Piranhas are famous for their sharp teeth and ability to strip their victims to the bone in a mad feeding frenzy. Less well known is their amazing vision. Piranhas live in waters that seem dark and murky to the human eye, but because of their ability to pick out certain kinds of light, they can still see clearly in inky black waters.

Red-bellied piranha

ANGLER FISH

The flashing dorsal fin of the deep-sea angler fish (*below*) dangles above its mouth and serves as bait for other fish.

CAVE FISH

Some fish live in underground caves where there is no light. With no use for its eyes in the gloom, one Mexican fish has lost its sight (below). To find its way around, it relies on a system of sensors that run along its body. Each sensor consists of sensitive hairs attached to a jellylike rod, which bends in the direction of the water moving around it. In this way, the fish can pick up any disturbances in the water caused by predators or prey.

29

FINDING OUT MORE

Amphibians are animals that live part of their life in water and part on land. They include frogs, toads, newts, and salamanders. Their skins have no scales and let water in and out.

Burrows are holes dug in the ground by animals for shelter or defense.

Camouflage is the markings and colors on an animal that help it to hide. For example, some moths look like leaves so they can hide in bushes.

Carnivores are animals that eat meat. Animals that eat only plants are called herbivores.

Cold-blooded creatures, such as reptiles, have a body that remains at the same temperature as the air or water around them. Unlike mammals, they cannot cool down by sweating. So, to avoid getting too hot, many reptiles are active at night, especially those that live in the dry heat of the desert.

Colony is the name for a group of animals living together, such as bats, ants, or termites. Colonies may have just a few members — or many millions.

Diurnal describes animals that are active only during the day — the opposite to nocturnal.

A Long Night's Sleep
During winter, when food supplies are short, some mammals go to sleep, not just for a night, but for a few months. Their heartbeat and breathing slow down, and they live off fat in their bodies. This is known as hibernation.

Echolocation is a system of echoes used by bats to find their way in darkness. These echoes come from high-pitched squeaks bats make while they are flying. From these echoes, the bats work out where objects are around them, such as trees and prey. Most of their squeaks are so high that humans cannot hear them.

Glands are parts of the body that produce special chemicals. One gland in human bodies, for example, produces the chemical adrenaline. When we get excited or upset, this chemical makes our hearts beat faster.

Grubs are the young of certain insects, such as beetles and bees.

Infrared is a sort of light that the human eye cannot see. All objects give off infrared rays, which increase as they get hotter. Special cameras pick up these rays and can follow animals in the dark by tracking their warm bodies. In the same way, some snakes have special pits that allow them to track the warm bodies of their prey.

Insects are animals with six legs and a body made up of three parts — the head, thorax (chest), and abdomen (rear). Most insects also have wings.

Mammals are warm-blooded animals with backbones. They have large brains and sharp senses, and communicate by actions, sounds, and smells. They also feed milk to their young.

THE EYE TEST

Eyes are an important tool for nighttime creatures. Some have large eyes to let in more light, others have a special layer called the tapetum that bounces light back into the eye. All the eyes below are from creatures that appear in this book. Can you find who they belong to? (All answers to questions on this spread can be found at the bottom of page 32).

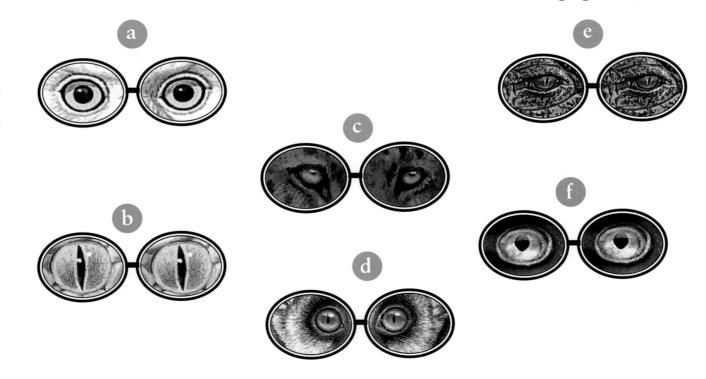

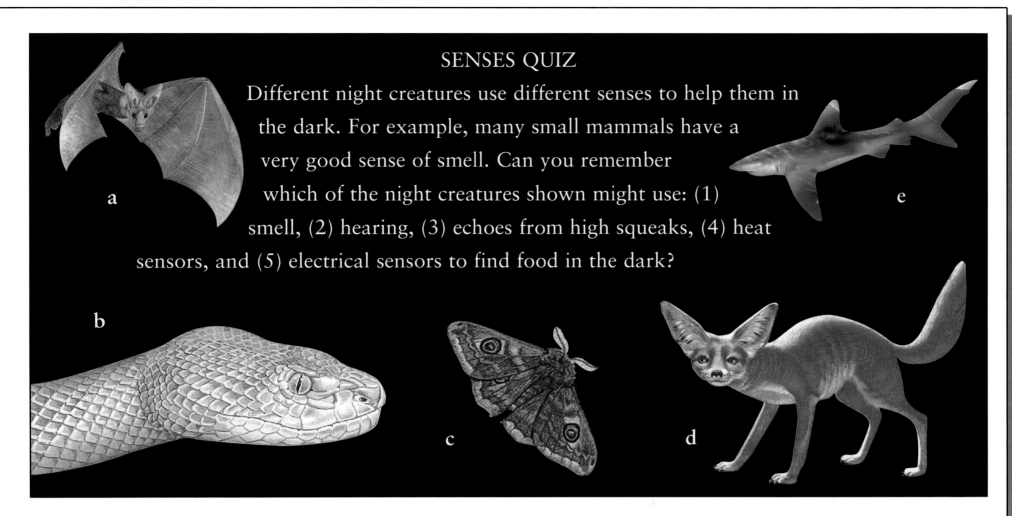

SENSES QUIZ

Different night creatures use different senses to help them in the dark. For example, many small mammals have a very good sense of smell. Can you remember which of the night creatures shown might use: (1) smell, (2) hearing, (3) echoes from high squeaks, (4) heat sensors, and (5) electrical sensors to find food in the dark?

Marsupials are mammals, such as kangaroos, that bring up their young in a pouch. Possums, koalas, wallabies, and wombats are all marsupials.

Monotremes are a group of mammals that lay eggs.

Nectar is the sweet liquid inside flowers. It attracts insects, such as moths and some bats at night, and bees during the day.

Organs are the major parts of an animal or plant and have a particular job. For example, the brain is the organ of thinking, and the stomach is the organ of digestion.

Predators are animals that hunt, kill, and eat other animals for food. They can be big, like lions, or small, like praying mantises.

Prey are animals that are hunted and killed for food.

Reptiles are animals with backbones and dry, scaly skins. Reptiles include lizards, snakes, crocodiles, and turtles.

Rodents are small mammals such as rats and mice. Many are active at night to avoid predators.

Warm-blooded animals are creatures, like many mammals, that can keep their bodies at the same temperature in hot or cold weather. Chemical reactions inside warm-blooded bodies create heat. Mammals keep in the heat with layers of fat and fur. When they get too hot, many mammals produce sweat. This liquid evaporates and cools the body.

NOISY NIGHTS

At night, the air is full of strange noises as animals call to each other in the dark. For example, nightingales sing to attract a mate, and wolves howl to "talk" with each other. But many animals keep as quiet as possible because they don't want to be eaten or because they want to sneak up on their prey without warning. Which of these animals are quiet at night, and which are noisy?

INDEX

ANSWERS TO QUIZZES ON PAGES 30–31

The Eye Test: a = snowy owl (page 20), b = snake (page 23), c = leopard (page 8), d = bushbaby (page 16), e = sea crocodile (page 22), f = sand tiger shark (page 28). *Senses Quiz*: a = 3 the ghost bat uses echoes from high squeaks to fly in the dark, b = 4 some snakes have heat sensors to find warm-blooded prey at night, c = 1 some moths' antennae can pick up smells from several miles away, d = 2 fennec foxes have very sharp hearing suited to the quiet deserts where they live, e = 5 sharks have electrical sensors in their snout that can detect the movement of other animals in the water. *Noisy Nights Quiz*: a = grasshoppers rub their legs together to produce a loud chirping sound to attract a mate, b = howler monkeys cry out to tell other howlers to keep away, c = frogs croak loudly to attract a mate, d = leopards are very quiet so they can creep up on their prey, e = snakes also slither silently to sneak up on their prey.